Exploring Materials

Glass

Abby Colich

Raintree is an imprint of Capstone Global Library Limited, a company incorporated in England and Wales having its registered office at 7 Pilgrim Street, London, EC4V 6LB Registered company number: 6695582

www.raintreepublishers.co.uk
myorders@raintreepublishers.co.uk

Text © Capstone Global Library Limited 2014
First published in hardback in 2014
Paperback edition first published in 2015
The moral rights of the proprietor have been asserted.

Edited by Abby Colich, Dan Nunn, and Catherine Veitch
Designed by Marcus Bell
Picture research by Tracy Cummins
Production by Victoria Fitzgerald
Originated by Capstone Global Library Ltd
Printed and bound in China

ISBN 978 1 4062 6331 2 (hardback)
17 16 15 14 13
10 9 8 7 6 5 4 3 2 1

ISBN 978 1 4062 6339 8 (paperback)
18 17 16 15 14
10 9 8 7 6 5 4 3 2 1

British Library Cataloguing in Publication Data
Colich, Abby.
Glass. – (Exploring materials)
620.1'44-dc23
A full catalogue record for this book is available from the British Library.

Acknowledgements
We would like to thank the following for permission to reproduce photographs: Corbis pp. 9, 23b (© Marc Romanelli/Blend Images); Getty Images pp. 10, 23c (© Philip and Karen Smith), p19 (© Mark Williamson); Photo Researchers p. 8 (© RIA Novosti / Science Source); Shutterstock pp. 4 (© Ingrid Maasik), 5 (© sritangphoto), 6a (© action studio), 6b (© Peter Hansen), 6c (© Sofiaworld), 6d (© lisasaadphotography), 7 (© Dudarev Mikhail), 11 (© Tatiana Popova), 12 (© Tom Wang), 13 (© Ramon grosso dolarea), 14 (© shadow216), 15 (© Galushko Sergey), 16 (© Tristanbm), 17 (© Diego Cervo), 18 (© Rostislav Glinsky), 20 (© Dhoxax), 21 (© LouLouPhotos), 22 (Anteromite, © akiyoko, © threeseven), 23a (© Diego Cervo).

Front cover photograph of a schoolgirl looking through a magnifying glass reproduced with permission of age footstock (© WAVEBREAKMEDIA LTD).

Back cover photograph reproduced with permission of Shutterstock (© Ramon grosso dolarea).

We would like to thank Valarie Akerson, Nancy Harris, Dee Reid, and Diana Bentley for their assistance in the preparation of this book.

Every effort has been made to contact copyright holders of material reproduced in this book. Any omissions will be rectified in subsequent printings if notice is given to the publisher.

Contents

What is glass?

Glass is a material.

Materials are what things are
made from.

Glass has many uses.

We use glass to make many different things.

Where does glass come from?

Glass is made by people.

People melt sand and other
materials together to make glass.

Glass can be recycled or reused.

Recycled glass can be used to make new things.

What is glass like?

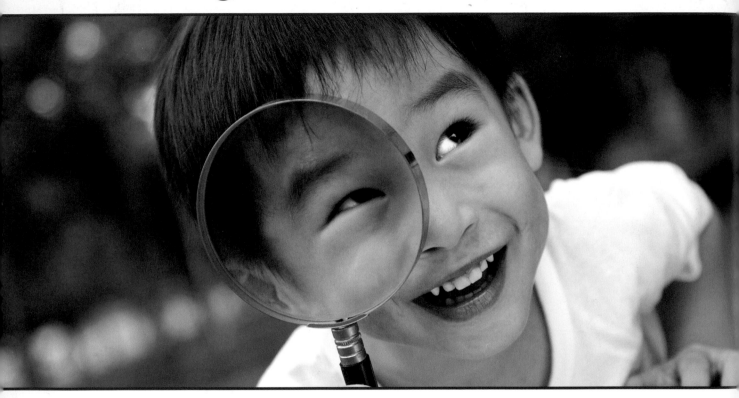

Glass can be clear.

Glass can be coloured.

Glass is hard and smooth.

Glass can break. Broken glass
is sharp.

How do we use glass?

We drink from glass cups.

container →

We store food in glass containers.

Many windows are made of glass.

Some buildings are made of glass.

People wear glasses to help them see.

People use glass to make art.

Quiz

Which of these things are made of glass?

Answer on page 24.

Picture glossary

 **container** something used to store things

 **melt** when something becomes soft and runny as it is heated

 **recycle** make used items into new things

Index

The **glass cups (a)** and **marbles (c)** are made of glass.

Notes for parents and teachers

Before reading

Ask children if they have heard the term "material" and what they think it means. Reinforce the concept of materials. Explain that all objects are made from different materials. A material is something that takes up space and can be used to make other things. Ask the children to give examples of different materials. These may include glass, plastic, and metal.

To get children interested in the topic, ask if they know what glass is. Identify any misconceptions they may have. Ask them to think about whether their ideas might change as the book is read.

After reading

- Check to see if any of the identified misconceptions have changed.
- Show the children examples of glass, including marbles, glasses, and a drinking glass.
- Pass the glass objects round the children. Ask them to describe the properties of each object. Is the glass coloured or clear? Heavy or light? Ask them to name other items made from glass.